FIRST SPORT

SKATEBOARDING

James Nixon

Photography by Bobby Humphrey

W

FRANKLIN WATTS
LONDON·SYDNEY

First published in 2014
by Franklin Watts

Franklin Watts
338 Euston Road
London NW1 3BH

Franklin Watts Australia
Level 17/207 Kent Street
Sydney, NSW 2000

Series Editor: Julia Bird
Planning and production by Discovery Books Ltd
Editor: James Nixon
Series designer: Ian Winton
Commissioned photography: Bobby Humphrey
Picture credits: Alamy: pp. 8 (PCN Photography),
23 (epa european pressphoto agency b. v.);
Shutterstock: pp. 3 (Rob Marmion), 9 top (littleny).

The author, packager and publisher would like to thank Creation Skate
Park, Birmingham, for their help and participation in this book.

Dewey number 796.2'2
ISBN: 978 1 4451 2634 0
Library ebook ISBN: 978 1 4451 2638 8

Printed in China

Franklin Watts is a division of Hachette Children's Books,
an Hachette UK company.
www.hachette.co.uk

Contents

What is skateboarding?

Skateboarding is one of the most exciting sports around. Skaters ride on a board and perform lots of eye-catching tricks.

Learning moves on a skateboard takes skill and bravery. There are competitions to test your skills, but most skaters simply ride their boards for fun.

The gear you need

The top of a skateboard is called the **deck.** It is covered in a special tape to help your feet grip.

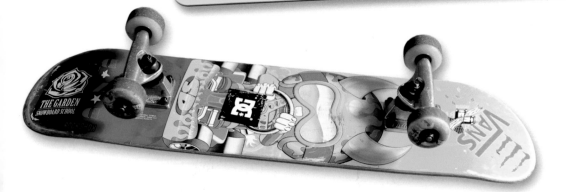

DECK
the wooden platform on a skateboard that skaters stand on

The wheels are made from tough plastic that rolls smoothly and quickly.

Skating can be dangerous. You should protect yourself in case you fall. You should wear knee pads and elbow pads, as well as a helmet.

Skate shoes are comfortable and have soles that give you good grip.

Helmet

Elbow pad

Knee pad

Skate shoes

Where to skate

Most towns have concrete spaces where skaters can practise their moves. To stay safe, do not skate anywhere that is close to traffic.

Many places also have specially built skate parks.

These contain ramps, **bowls** and **rails** that skaters can use to show off their tricks.

BOWL
A concrete or wooden area of a skate park shaped like a bowl

RAIL
A straight, metal bar set off the ground

9

Before you learn any tricks, you must get used to riding a skateboard. Put one foot on the board and push yourself along with your other foot.

When you feel ready, put both feet on the board.

Don't worry if you find it difficult to start with. Skateboarding needs a lot of practice, as well as good balance!

To stop skating, just put one foot back down on the ground.

Making turns

To turn the board, lean the way you want to move. Steering a skateboard through a bend is called **carving**.

Gaining speed and flow on your skateboard is just as much fun as doing tricks.

CARVE
lean your body to turn a skateboard in a different direction

Leaning back a little on your heels steers the board one way.

Leaning forward towards your toes carves the board in the other direction.

13

The ollie

The first trick a skateboarder should learn is the 'ollie'.

This is when a skater leaps in the air along with their board.

To do an ollie, crouch down on the board. As you start to stand up, push down hard on the **tail** of the board with your back foot (below).

TAIL
the back part of a skateboard deck that curves upwards

Then guide the board up into the air with your front foot.

Flip tricks

Once you have learned the ollie there are lots of other moves you can try. Flip-tricks are like ollies, but the board is flipped over in mid-air.

To flip the skateboard over, you can flick the **nose** of the board with your heel or toes.

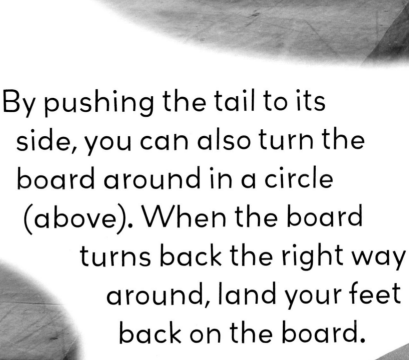

NOSE
the front part of a skateboard deck that curves upwards

By pushing the tail to its side, you can also turn the board around in a circle (above). When the board turns back the right way around, land your feet back on the board.

17

Grinds and slides

Grinds and slides are more difficult moves. Grinding is when a skater slides the board's **trucks** along the edge of a step, rail or ramp.

Truck

TRUCKS
the metal bars that connect the wheels to the deck on a skateboard

Grinds can be done using the tail or nose of the board.

Skidding the middle of the board along a surface is called a slide. Only skaters who have great board control can pull these moves off.

Grabs

Grabs are lots of fun. This is when skaters grab the board in different ways in mid-air.

A grab lets you perform twists and turns during a jump because the board is under control.

Different types of grabs have different names.

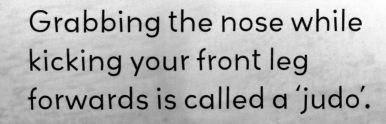

Grabbing the nose while kicking your front leg forwards is called a 'judo'.

Holding the back of the board between your legs like this is called a 'melon'!

On the halfpipe

Top skaters take part in competitions on massive, steep ramps called **halfpipes.**

Skaters build up huge speeds and perform tricks such as spins at amazing heights. To do a '360' trick the skater must do one full twist in the air.

HALFPIPE
A large up-and-down ramp shaped like the bottom half of a pipe

Skaters take turns on the halfpipes and perform their moves in front of **judges.** To get the top scores, skaters have to land their boards perfectly back down on the ramp.

JUDGE
a person who decides the results of a competition

Index